Richard Brown's
New England

Richard Brown's New England

TEXT AND PHOTOGRAPHY BY
RICHARD W. BROWN

Introduction by Castle Freeman, Jr.

FIREFLY BOOKS

A FIREFLY BOOK

Published by Firefly Books 1996

Cataloguing-in-Publication Data

Brown, Richard, 1945-
    Richard Brown's New England

ISBN 1-55209-070-1

1. New England - Pictorial works.   2. New England - Description and travel.
I. Title   II. Title: New England.

F5.B76 1996   974' .043'0222   C96-930952-X

Design by Susan McClellan

Published by
Firefly Books Ltd.
3680 Victoria Park Avenue
Willowdale, Ontario
Canada M2H 3K1

Published in the U.S. by
Firefly Books (U.S.) Inc.
P.O. Box 1338, Ellicott Station
Buffalo, New York 14205

Printed and bound in Canada by
Friesens
Altona, Manitoba

Printed on acid-free paper

Frontispiece: ACADIA COASTLINE, MAINE, 1980

Page 6: APPROACHING STORM, PEACHAM, VERMONT, 1976

For Susan and Willa

INTRODUCTION

CASTLE FREEMAN, JR.

EVERY GOOD BOOK IS ITS OWN EPITOME, AND THEREFORE, THE BEST introduction to the pictures in *Richard Brown's New England* may be not an appreciation of them by a longtime admirer, not a written account at all, but simply one of the pictures themselves. I have in mind the photograph facing this page. Take a moment and examine it with me.

We are standing on a hill looking over a narrow valley. Down there, maybe a mile away, is a little village: a single church steeple and a clutch of white houses. Between our hill and the village are green fields, some pretty large, some apparently no more than a few acres. The fields are divided by tree lines that seem to converge on a house on the outskirts of the village to the left — perhaps, in part, a trick of perspective. Among the fields are two farmsteads, one to the left, one to the right; you can see their long barns. In the fields between the farm on the left and the village, white dots are just visible. They must be sheep.

It's summertime. A thunderstorm is passing over the valley. The sky, which in fact takes up more than half the picture's space, is an ominous dark boil of seething storm clouds. The repose of the valley and its village is in contrast to the violence of the sky above them, but at the same time, the valley participates in the storm, especially through the weird livid light that seems to drench the entire scene.

The picture both accepts and declines the drama — and indeed the beauty — of the world it shows. As a response to its subject, it is ambiguous. The result is a division of feeling that is characteristic of the photographs of Richard Brown and that may be their most eloquent expression of the spirit of the place that is their setting.

For anyone who knows the northern New England hill country where many of these photographs were taken and who also knows the way that country is commonly portrayed, these pictures are remarkable first of all for their restraint. In a landscape that is often more than grand enough, the photographer resists grandeur. He resists the sublime. His landscapes are always on a human scale — even when they're not, so to speak. His mountain valleys and storm-filled skies are not the field for the spectacular forces of majestic, abstract Nature, or anyway, they are not that alone. They are also the homes of men and women and the places where their lives are lived. Nature in Richard Brown's pictures doesn't omit people and their concerns or dwarf them, as in some of the landscapes of the old Hudson River painters, for example. Rather, people and their jobs, their equipment, their houses, their kids, their livestock and pets are central and form the subjects of the majority of the photographs in this book, including those, like the one we have been considering, which seem to be the largest and most impersonal.

Not that the humane documentary impulse in these pictures is a mere strategy or device of this photographer. It's more as though he accepted that impulse as an essential part of a photographer's work. For in the camera, photographers surely have the best, most accurate instrument ever invented for answering the question, *What do people do?* In Richard Brown's pictures, they do a good deal of snow moving, logging, washing, plowing and other field preparation, sap-gathering, gardening and sitting around the kitchen. They also spend a lot of time with animals: cattle

JOHN AND GLADYS SOMERS
BARNET, VERMONT, 1977

EVENING CHORES, NORTHEAST KINGDOM, VERMONT, 1977

and oxen, horses, sheep, dogs and cats – and notably geese, a creature for which this photographer seems to have an abiding affection.

These pictures, then, are full of straightforward curiosity about what people are up to. But Richard Brown's documentaries, like his landscapes, are complex and imply a kind of split in the photographer's attention and therefore in our own as we look at the pictures and reflect upon them. For however close his camera comes to the lives and doings of the people who are his subjects, it is never quite familiar. There is always a certain distance, a certain privacy that has to do with the way the photographer's subjects seem to react to his transaction with them. The men and women in Richard Brown's pictures, as they go about their business, don't pretend the camera isn't there, but neither do they do much to accommodate it. The relationship between them and the photographer (and therefore between them and the viewer) is never intimate, but neither is it formal, posed or stereotyped. Finally, the relationship is respectful – hence the unusual reserve of the most successful of these pictures: they seem to contain more than they reveal.

I HAVE SUGGESTED THAT RICHARD BROWN'S PHOTOGRAPHS ARE NOT EXACTLY what they seem. There is more to them than meets the eye, you might say (which, when you think about it, is a pretty peculiar observation to make about a picture). His landscapes withhold a conventional celebration of Nature, and his pictures of people resist easy familiarity. You would expect his work to be austere, therefore, or solemn. It is neither, and that is the most remarkable achievement of these pictures. This photographer is perfectly well aware of the traditional New England epiphanies, and he doesn't neglect them. The riches of his subject matter and his enjoyment of them are evident, especially in his use of light and color and in the smaller pictures that resemble still lifes.

The light that Richard Brown has discovered in many of his most memorable pictures is familiar to anyone who has passed through New England, especially in fall or winter, the region's sovereign seasons. In these pictures, the yellow leaf-filtered daylight of autumn and the two best kinds of winter light — cold gray and hard, distant blue — are so striking as nearly to seem the true subjects. It's a painterly way of using light. artful, subtly exaggerated, almost antique.

Apart from the colors produced outdoors by sunlight, the most characteristic color in these pictures is a bright, loud red, seen in these pages in shirts, suspenders, tractors, poppies, rose hips, tomatoes and even in Santa Claus's suit. This red dash, for Richard Brown, is the pepper in the stew, serving to cut or relieve pictures that, without it, would be too subdued. It's often there for humor, an antic burst of high spirits in a world that has a use for them.

Another, quieter form of high spirits is to be seen in the small compositions of leaves, stones, ferns, tree branches and moving water and in some of the pictures of animals. In their minute scale, the most intimate of these pictures attain the rapt abstraction of a Japanese garden. They allow the photographer and the viewer to enter their scenery by forgetting it. The still lifes bring the landscape full circle.

Altogether, these pictures express a very specific view of their New England setting, not only from their choice of subject matter, light and color but even more from the ambiguity or complexity of feeling that they bring to it. The pictures are benign and peaceful, optimistic and well able to enjoy the beauty of their corner of Earth. But they are also worldly, measured, rigorous and grown-up. They have few illusions, or anyway, they have only the illusions they choose. It is in that open-eyed vision, particularly, that Richard Brown's photographs are of a piece with the land and the life they invite us to behold. .

Richard Brown's
New England

We New Englanders have mixed feelings about foliage season. We don't want to admit that this annual extravagance stirs us to the marrow. We complain about the influx of gawkers; we say the color isn't as good this year. We grumble, knowing this sudden blaze of glory means the end of the easy times; only shorter, darker, colder days to come. Yet we pause and drink in each color-splashed hillside when others aren't looking.

LEAF PATTERN, WHITE MOUNTAINS, NEW HAMPSHIRE, 1988

HIDDEN COVE

ACADIA, MAINE, 1995

BIRCHES

COLRAIN, MASSACHUSETTS

1980

More often than not, mornings in October mean fog. The best kind is fleeting, just filling the low places at dawn, then riding up over tree lines and ridges in the warming air. But sometimes it's everywhere — heavy, opaque and sedentary, hanging around past noon like an unwelcome slothful guest.

EAST HILL, PEACHAM, VERMONT, 1971

INDIAN SUMMER
NEWARK, VERMONT, 1974

Late fall in New England is an acquired taste – such drabness after all that leaf color. It's a bare-bones time of the year, when old walls reappear and the land's true contours are revealed. Everything is earth-toned – shades of burnt umber, raw sienna and yellow ocher. Even at midday, shadows are long and deep, yet field stubble and tree branches are still gilded by the low sunlight.

HAUNTED HOUSE, MARSHFIELD, VERMONT, 1979

HAY-SCENTED FERNS, HEATH, MASSACHUSETTS, 1970

SPREADING MANURE

KIRBY, VERMONT, 1973

W HEN I FIRST MOVED TO VERMONT'S
Northeast Kingdom, there was still
a generation of farmers holding onto the past.
It was a combination of isolation, stubbornness
and survival. Improvements and new machinery
required income that these thin fields would
never yield, so these diehards did without —
and thumbed their noses at progress.

Left: GRAVESTONE CARVING
SUNDERLAND, RHODE ISLAND
1989

Every New England community has its ancient burial plot, with creaking gates and tilted stones. Judging from the dates chiseled in granite or marble, our forebears lived either very long or very short lives. Weatherworn inscriptions harp on our mortality: *"As you are now, so once was I."* But in the face of death, these people held their faith. They believed in angels.

Right: CEMETERY
NORTH HAVEN, MAINE, 1974

SUNSET

AROOSTOOK COUNTY, MAINE

1979

NOVEMBER IS THE DARKEST MONTH — in feeling, if not in actuality. Afternoon seems to end before it has barely begun. There is a hurried quality to the daylight hours — a sense that a great deal must be done before each premature nightfall. We have a squirrel-like preoccupation with the cold and snow that will descend soon enough from this lowering purple sky.

Left: WOODPILE

RANDOLPH, VERMONT, 1976

ONE OF RURAL LIFE'S GREATEST PLEASURES
— and nuisances — is heating with wood.
A woodstove radiates warmth like no other
form of heat. However, you can't take it for
granted like an oil furnace — you have to have
a relationship with your stove. You have to
humor it, feed it constantly like a fussy cat,
adjust the dampers, poke at it and coax it back
to life in the small hours of the morning with
bits of kindling and crumpled-up junk mail.
Old-timers pep theirs up with a stiff shot of
kerosene. The black iron pings and groans, the
burning wood shifts inside with a reassuring
sigh, and the pleasing pungency of woodsmoke
faintly laces the air.

Right: GIRL AND COOKSTOVE

NORTHEAST KINGDOM, VERMONT

1988

Left: WOODBINE

DANIELSON, CONNECTICUT

1995

Right: CORN STUBBLE

CALEDONIA COUNTY, VERMONT

1983

CHOATE'S BARNYARD, NORTHEAST KINGDOM, VERMONT, 1976

BEN THRESHER'S

BARNET CENTER, VERMONT, 1978

THE FARMER WHO SOLD ME MY FARM insisted on selling it "stocked" with an ancient draft horse and three bred heifers. Within a year, I was a regular Old McDonald. A venerable Yankee barn may be a thing of beauty, but without animals, it is without purpose and life.

PLOWING OUT, EAST PEACHAM, VERMONT, 1979

THE INITIAL DUSTING OF SNOW IS A NOVELTY. It has a certain Currier and Ives charm; but you pray it won't stay, and you can squeeze out a few more weeks of life without boots and sodden cuffs and searching for the dog dish that the town plow buried. Then the real snow comes for good — smothering and bleaching the landscape with a foot or more of the damnable stuff. First you scowl at it for a while, then you relax and accept winter on its own terms. Now you can turn your back on the unraked leaves, the wood that didn't get put in and all the toys the children left out there — somewhere. You eye the vast, white all-hiding sea that laps at your door and grin.

FARM KIDS, BARNET, VERMONT, 1979

EAST HILL

PEACHAM, VERMONT, 1971

THE NEW ENGLAND COUNTRYSIDE IS
one of the few places on Earth where,
for a time, people improved the look of things.
The harmonious pattern of cleared land and
forest, of pasture, mowing, fencerow and woodlot is infinitely more appealing to my eye than
the forest primeval – and equally rare.

RED BARN

MARSHFIELD, VERMONT, 1979

IN WINTER, THE BARN IS A GREENHOUSE for animals, an oasis in a desert of blinding whiteness, a domesticated Noah's Ark, solidly anchored in a five-month flood of snow.

JOHN SOMERS AND HEIFERS

BARNET, VERMONT, 1978

FIRSTBORN

NORTHEAST KINGDOM, VERMONT

1988

T HERE SHOULD BE A SPECIAL WORD
for the contentment that comes from
keeping winter safely at bay. The warmth of
a snug old farmhouse and the joy of a new
child are never more fully savored than when
a blizzard rages outside.

BEGINNING STORM, MOSQUITOVILLE, VERMONT, 1981

Left: SHOVELING THE ROOF
NORTHEAST KINGDOM, VERMONT
1979

Right: THE FLOCK
PEACHAM, VERMONT, 1972

LOGGING AT CARPENTER'S
CABOT, VERMONT, 1979

Even the kind of cold that makes
snow squeak under the horses' hooves
and a man's breath freeze in his beard won't
keep a logger from going into the woods.

FEEDING TIME, WASHINGTON COUNTY, VERMONT, 1988

CATCHING SNOWFLAKES

PEACHAM, VERMONT, 1980

AT THE CLOSE OF A DECEMBER DAY, THERE is a unique indigo light which lingers like an afterthought, or perhaps an apology, left by a weary sun that has made such a meager effort.

CHARLES BAGELY
PASSUMPSIC, VERMONT, 1988

Behold, a freelance Santa Claus and a country pastor, contrary voices of the season, purveyors of the secular and the sacred, the yin and the yang of our most incongruous and beloved holiday – Christmas.

REVEREND BLANKENSHIP

PEACHAM, VERMONT, 1988

THE VILLAGES PICTURED ON CHRISTMAS cards are invariably the kind of quint-essential New England village shown here: a steepled white church with dark green shutters, neat clapboard houses and time-stained barns nestled in a valley. While these villages may have mangers, shepherds and perhaps a self-proclaimed wise man or two, it is their enduring sense of peace that makes these small towns our Christmas icons.

Above: BOBCAT, HOLDERNESS, NEW HAMPSHIRE, 1988   *Right:* WOODLOT, LITTLETON, NEW HAMPSHIRE, 1983

BOBCATS ARE SHY AND ELUSIVE, BUT NOT uncommon. I often hear their hair-raising shrieks in the dead of night. Neighbors with more acute, or imaginative, hearing than mine say they have heard other animal screams so blood-curdling that they could only have been made by a catamount. The forests of New England are being reclaimed by their rightful predatory heirs.

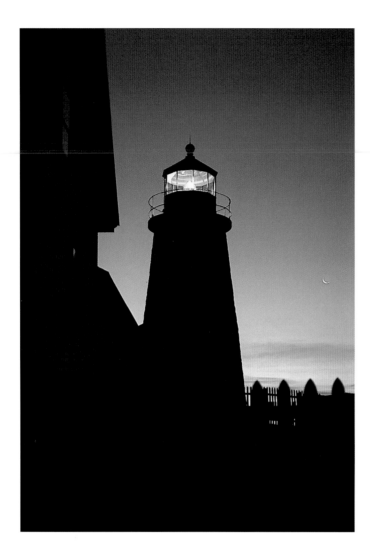

CRESCENT MOON
PEMAQUID POINT, MAINE, 1990

WINTER EMPHASIZES THE EDWARD Hopper sense of loneliness and isolation inherent in so much of New England's architecture. A limitless cobalt sky sheds an icy blue light on each clapboard and shingle with razor-edged clarity and cold indifference.

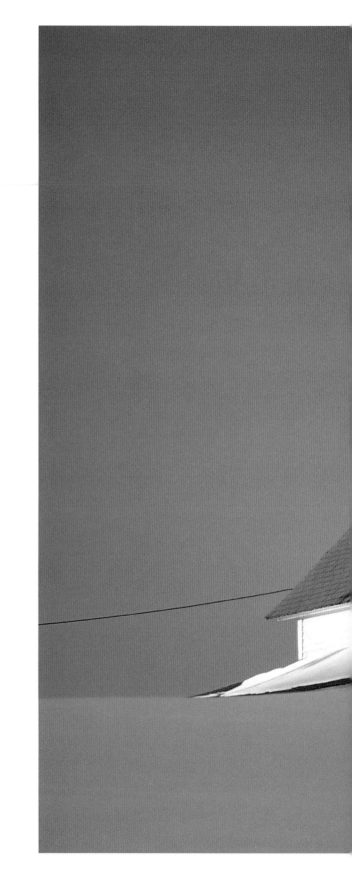

FARMHOUSE AND SNOW, PEACHAM, VERMONT, 1972

Left: FARMALL TRACTOR

CABOT, VERMONT, 1980

Right: CHARLES CHOATE

BARNET, VERMONT, 1987

Left: ARBORVITAE

CONCORD, MASSACHUSETTS, 1981

SNOWY OWLS ARE WINTER VISITORS FROM the Arctic regions of northernmost Canada. They fly down for a few months to get out of the cold, relatively speaking. New England is their Palm Beach, their Boca Raton. Their resemblance to snow is uncanny, as if formed from that element and brought to life by a white-bearded sorcerer in a child's winter tale.

Right: SNOWY OWL

WOODSTOCK, VERMONT, 1987

ICE SKATING

CALEDONIA COUNTY, VERMONT

1981

TELEPHONE CALL

BARNET, VERMONT, 1977

TOWN MEETING

BARNET, VERMONT, 1977

T HE FIRST TUESDAY IN MARCH IS TOWN
meeting day – democracy in its purest
form. Town officials are elected or thrown out,
budgets are appropriated, and a prodigious
number of casseroles are consumed. As this
meeting coincides with the advent of mud
season, the condition of the town's roads and
the efficacy of the road commissioner are often
called into question. Tempers flare, and a good
deal of gavel-pounding ensues. I recall one of
our former commissioner's last official words:
"When you can show me the flat side of a rock,
I'll get your roads smooth!"

GRETCHEN'S PORCH
PEACHAM, VERMONT, 1981

In Vermont, we call it "cabin fever." In Maine, it's known as "woods queer." It's what happens in March when you live in an old farmhouse on a backwoods dirt road, snow- and mud-bound for weeks on end, and there hasn't been a sunny day in living memory. The best antidote is a trip to Tahiti, but most of us just grumble or curse. We step outside, hoping to catch the slightest scent of warmth in the wind or to see whether the laundry is finally dry.

WASHDAY, NORTHEAST KINGDOM, VERMONT, 1979

FIRST THAW

PIERMONT, NEW HAMPSHIRE

1991

When spring first arrives, it's not a pretty sight. Those of us who are foolish enough to venture forth, or have no choice, become true connoisseurs of mud, attuned to its every nuance and subtlety at each slough in the road. Large water-covered quagmires require a leap of faith and an unrelenting foot on the accelerator. What lies beneath is best left to ignorance, and any hint of indecision leads to certain disaster. The less foolhardy wait until evening, when it all freezes again.

STUART'S TEAM

CALEDONIA COUNTY, VERMONT

1973

MAKING MAPLE SYRUP IS THE BEST excuse for keeping draft horses or oxen on the farm. They actually do a better job of sap-gathering than machinery. A well-trained team doesn't need to be told what to do. The challenge is keeping up with them.

YOKE OF OXEN, PLAINFIELD, VERMONT, 1976

Left: GATHERING SAP

BARNET, VERMONT, 1979

Sugaring is a damp business. Pant legs and mittens become sodden from floundering through waterlogged drifts. Clouds of steam rise from the broad backs of the horses as they jolt and career through the woods. The air is alive with the smells of hemlock and wet harness, of saturated leaves under the snow and of the delicate, exotic scent of maple steam rising over the sugarhouse, where the sap madly boils and froths.

Right: SUGARHOUSE INTERIOR

BARNET, VERMONT, 1979

Left: CONTENTED CAT
NORTHEAST KINGDOM, VERMONT
1980

Right: SPRING HARROWING
WEST BARNET, VERMONT, 1977

NEW LEAVES, THE BERKSHIRES, MASSACHUSETTS, 1984

THE SWIFT PROGRESS OF THE NEW season is measured by the resurrection of once familiar sounds: the drumming of rain on the tin roof, the rush of running water replacing mute ice, the keening trill of peepers and the achingly pure notes of the white-throated sparrow that linger in the warm air.

SPRING RUNOFF, BETHEL, MAINE, 1986

GREEN HILLS

CALEDONIA COUNTY, VERMONT

1975

V ERMONT REDEEMS HER NAME EACH
May. She doesn't hold back. She exhausts
her gaudiest options: chartreuse for tender new
maple and poplar leaves, an intense lime for the
haze of corn pushing through the corduroy of
plowed ground. The fluorescent shimmering
of young growth radiates from the land.

SHEEP SHEARING

FOSTER, RHODE ISLAND, 1987

EWE AND LAMB

HUDSON, MASSACHUSETTS 1985

SHEARING IS AN ANNUAL INDIGNITY suffered by sheep. The fleece, creamy yellow and heavy with lanolin, lies in a woolen pile at the shearer's feet. The naked ewe rises shakily, emits a hoarse *baa* and, with three or four bounding leaps, rejoins the flock. Even her own lambs don't recognize this pathetic beast with shrunken body and giant head. They recoil in horror. She retreats to the barn. All is vanity.

Left: PLANTING PEAS
PEACHAM, VERMONT, 1979

Right: HOWE FARM
TUNBRIDGE, VERMONT, 1976

FARM COLLIE
NORTH DANVILLE, VERMONT
1973

JESSICA AND GEORGE
PEACHAM, VERMONT, 1979

"ARE YOUR GEESE UGLY?" A YOUNG visitor once asked. At first, I thought she was referring to their appearance, and I was mildly insulted. Then I realized she used the word in its old-fashioned sense, as in "likely to cause inconvenience or discomfort." George, as I named this particular goose, was indeed a miserable and ungrateful fowl. I tenderly nursed him through incubation and infancy only to be repaid by his constant and malicious sneak attacks whenever my back was turned. George caused a lot of inconvenience. Not only was he ugly, he didn't look very pretty either.

THE FURROWED GROUND SHINES WITH
the polish of the plow. Evening light
catches the rising dust and the blackflies
swarming about the horses' flanks and massive
fetlocks. The farmer walks to ease the team's
burden. Robins, thrushes, even fiery tanagers
soon follow in his wake, like seagulls behind a
trawler, as the fat white grubs spill from the
turned earth.

CRAB APPLE TREE, MARLBORO, VERMONT, 1992

THE BEST NEW ENGLAND GARDENS HAVE that late-19th-century feeling of unstudied exuberance. "Grandmother's gardens," we call them, where heady masses of old-fashioned flowers spill over walkways and smother arbors. They are forever associated in our minds with ample-bosomed matrons wearing white dresses and large, plumed hats.

COTTAGE GARDEN, WEST BARNET, VERMONT, 1993

PASTORAL HILLSIDE

ORLEANS COUNTY, VERMONT

1982

Left: SUSANNAH AND LILACS
PEACHAM, VERMONT, 1982

Nothing evokes an old Yankee homestead like an ancient lilac standing roof-high in full and redolent bloom. It is as quintessentially New England as the song of the hermit thrush or the scent of burning leaves. Each Memorial Day, this not-quite-purple, not-quite-violet flower marks a turning point. In the local cemetery, children place sprigs of lilac on the graves of veterans, as an old soldier in an antiquated uniform plays taps, and spring imperceptibly turns to summer.

Right: MEMORIAL DAY
CALEDONIA COUNTY, VERMONT
1979

Left: DOE AND FAWN

SQUAM LAKE, NEW HAMPSHIRE

1979

JUNE IS WHEN THE BUNCHBERRY BLOOMS beneath Maine's dark firs. It is also when the first crop of hay gets cut and when white-tailed does drop their fawns. This latter coincidence is unfortunate. Deer prefer to hide their newborn offspring in the tall grass at the edge of a field, and mowing the first few swaths around the perimeter can be nerve-racking. Fawns that are a few days old make a startling bleat like a lamb and hightail it into the woods. But fawns that have just been born seem to think they're invisible. They lie there until you carefully scoop them up and place their heart-pounding bodies in a safer spot.

Right: BUNCHBERRY

NORTHEAST HARBOR, MAINE

1986

JUNE EVENING

BARNET, VERMONT, 1972

LOW TIDE

NAHANT, MASSACHUSETTS

1976

I HAVE GREAT RESPECT FOR THE MEN from Gloucester and Rockland who fish for lobsters and cod in wave-tossed boats. New England lore and legend are full of such seafaring men, but I am no Queequeg. I once attempted to row out in a small dory to a barely visible island. At the halfway point, the sea was vast, black and unfathomable. My puny craft tilted and plunged unmercifully. For a few transcendent moments, I was an old salt in a Winslow Homer painting, with the heaving waves obscuring all horizon and the cold spray crashing over the gunwales. Then terror and better judgment prevailed — I turned and rowed furiously back to shore. Let me poke about in tidal pools or bask on granite rocks with the waves gently lapping below. I like the sea with my legs on the land.

MOSQUITO POINT, MARTINSVILLE, MAINE, 1990

Above: RAKING HAY, CALEDONIA COUNTY, VERMONT, 1975   *Right:* THERON BOYD, QUECHEE, VERMONT, 1977

THERON BOYD AND HIS FARM WERE UNIQUE, a living glimpse into a century ago. He lived in a magnificent but crumbling Federal mansion, mowing his fields with a scythe and drawing his water from a well. When I visited, I felt awed, like an archaeologist encountering a living pharaoh. At Theron's, television didn't exist, or radio or electric lights — or, in fact, electricity. On the mantel in the kitchen, a half-dozen clocks ticked and chimed incessantly — but never simultaneously. I asked him once what time it was. With a cryptic look, he replied, "Your time or mine?"

CLEARING STORM, BROWNINGTON, VERMONT, 1985

SUNRISE, NORTHEAST KINGDOM, VERMONT, 1972

Left: MOSS GLEN FALLS
GRANVILLE, VERMONT, 1977

IT IS NO SLIGHT MIRACLE THAT HIDDEN
corners of New England remain pristine
and wild. Thoreau rejoiced in such modest but
inspiring surroundings over a century ago. He
found enough uncivilized territory in Concord,
Massachusetts, to build a squatter's cabin and
make a brilliant nuisance of himself. Self-
appointed observer of the New England wilds,
often on hands and knees with his journal and
"spyglass," he saw a Niagara in every waterfall
and a moon's eclipse in the markings of a luna
moth's lucent green wings.

Right: LUNA MOTH
HOG ISLAND, MAINE, 1989

SWEET PEAS

BARNET, VERMONT, 1979

WHEN WE ARE CHILDREN, SUMMER is an eternity — endless days of lazy warmth and cicadas singing, of swimming at the lake and pony rides and skinned knees. But when we have more life under our belts, we wonder how summer goes by so quickly. In the midst of its humid rush, we pause for a few moments to pick the sweet peas and keep the cat amused.

PONY RIDE, BARNET, VERMONT, 1982

EVENING POND

LAKEVILLE, CONNECTICUT

1982

A T DUSK, THE SURFACE OF THE POND
turns to lilac. Old-man bullfrogs belch
and moan, fireflies spangle the darkness, and
shadowy wings flicker and dart at the night.

WILD ROSE HIPS

NORTH HAVEN, MAINE, 1979

GAY HEAD, MARTHA'S VINEYARD, MASSACHUSETTS, 1975

Above: TUNBRIDGE FAIR, TUNBRIDGE, VERMONT, 1976   *Right:* GRETCHEN'S GARDEN, PEACHAM, VERMONT, 1984

IN SEPTEMBER, AFTER MONTHS OF BATTLING woodchucks, overzealous squash and other vagaries of the growing season, it is time to give the hoe a rest and celebrate a little. We clean up our children, our cattle and our vegetables and show them off at the fair.

SUSAN'S GARDEN

PEACHAM, VERMONT, 1982

THE YOUNG WOMAN WITH PERFECT BRAID heavy on her back carefully places the next-to-last tomato in the pail. The laggards will ripen on windowsills. We make them last, on the floor in the attic or wrapped in newspaper in the garage — whatever we can devise to prolong the taste of high summer. Each bite is a vindication of the genuine over the counterfeit. It will be late November before we again have to suffer those alien pink spheres from the grocery store.

GREEN TOMATOES

NORTHEAST KINGDOM, VERMONT

1983

WANDERING GEESE

PLAINFIELD, VERMONT, 1976

GREEN GIVES WAY TO ORANGE, AND A flock of domesticated geese satisfies its migratory urge with a stroll down the road. When their wild cousins surge overhead in great clamorous V's, they cock their heads and turn their beady eyes skyward in astonishment. A honking cheer breaks out amongst this earth-bound gaggle. The call of the wild still stirs their poor waddling souls.

RATTLESNAKE FERN

WHITE MOUNTAINS

NEW HAMPSHIRE

1979

MILKWEED

THE BERKSHIRES

MASSACHUSETTS

1979

JERSEY COWS, NORTHEAST KINGDOM, VERMONT, 1971

THE FENTONS

MIDDLETOWN SPRINGS, VERMONT

1984

THIS FARM AND THIS COUPLE SPEAK
with silent eloquence of a way of life,
now past, when it was possible to wrest a living
from two hundred bony acres and a dozen Jersey
cows the color of bronze.

BIRCH FOREST

ESSEX COUNTY, VERMONT

1979

Birches are pleasingly spooky; something more than sap may flow within their supple ranks. Movement is implied in their slender grace, white magic in the pallor of their chalky skin.

Left: BEACH DETAIL
CAPE ROSIER, MAINE, 1995

THE LEAVES OF THE SOFT MAPLE BLAZE
and fall. They scurry across a bouillabaisse
of mussels and periwinkles with each gust of
wind. Blueberry meadows turn scarlet. Their
rising tide of fire maroons a derelict house and
washes past the granite boulders in its path.

Right: BLUEBERRY FIELDS
BROOKSVILLE, MAINE, 1995

LIGHTHOUSE REFLECTION
PEMAQUID POINT, MAINE
1993

O NLY THE THIN MARGIN OF ROCKY
coast wrapped in fog and dark ever-
greens escapes the annual conflagration.

TOMBSTONES, PEACHAM, VERMONT, 1972

THE HIRED MAN

PLAINFIELD, VERMONT, 1976

Left: SPRUCE FOREST
ISLESBORO, MAINE, 1980

O N WET MORNINGS, THE WOODS ARE
filled with the unmistakable scent of fall:
the wintergreen smell of spruce and fir mingled
with the leathery tang of frostbitten ferns and
damp leafmold.

Right: INTERRUPTED FERNS
COLRAIN, MASSACHUSETTS, 1970

HILLS OF HOME

NORTHEAST KINGDOM, VERMONT

1973

W E NEED A LANDSCAPE WITH AN INNER
swell, a roll and a swagger – a horizon
that gives the eye some exercise and the mind a
place to wander.

Left: RAKE FACTORY BROOK
BARNET, VERMONT, 1980

Right: FUNGUS DETAIL
DARIEN, CONNECTICUT, 1974

FOGGY MORNING, MOSQUITOVILLE, VERMONT, 1982

FALLEN LEAVES
WHITINGHAM, VERMONT, 1970

THERE IS A TURNING POINT IN AUTUMN when there are more leaves on the ground than on the trees. They lie in crisp rustling pools. They swirl and roll in the wake of each passing car, until the weight of rain and age quiets their nervous movement.

How satisfying it must have been to lift and roll heavy stones out of the ground and build a wall based on the unquestioned assumption that all would stay as it was — that these sinuous barriers of granite would always fence in cattle and not trees.

NOVEMBER, CALEDONIA COUNTY, VERMONT, 1972

JACK-O'-LANTERNS, PEACHAM, VERMONT, 1980

IT IS THE PUMPKIN'S DESTINY TO BECOME either a pie or a jack-o'-lantern – golden brown ambrosia for our table or fire-eyed terror for our porch. Neither ages well.

A DAY DRAWS TO ITS CLOSE; THE LIGHT on the mountain is low and makes deep lavender shadows. The air grows chill, but at this time of year, it is not unwelcome. We take, perhaps, one last glance at these stubborn New England hills that have lent us their strength and endurance. We draw inside and center around the warmth of our kitchens and our children.

Right: MOUNT MOOSELAUKE
HAVERHILL, NEW HAMPSHIRE
1973

CAT AND STOVE

PEACHAM, VERMONT, 1982